THIS JOURNAL BELONGS TO

_____

ONE
Question
a Day
for KIDS

A THREE-YEAR JOURNAL

Castle Point Books
New York

WELCOME TO FUN, EVERYDAY JOURNALING!

It's time to get personal and express yourself! Inside you'll find cool questions ranging from lighthearted and funny to seriously deep. Find today's date and jot your answer down on the lines.

Each page includes three fill-in spaces so you can look back after three years and and see what has changed about you and what hasn't.

Hide this little book under your bed, toss it into your sock drawer, or stash it in the bottom of your backpack. This journal is a safe place to vent your feelings, explore your dreams, and share your opinions about the world. Just be YOU and let the words flow!

JANUARY 1

What is your New Year's wish?

YEAR: _____

_____

_____

_____

YEAR: _____

_____

_____

_____

YEAR: _____

_____

_____

_____

JANUARY 2

What is one thing you're looking
forward to this year?

YEAR: _____

_____

_____

_____

YEAR: _____

_____

_____

_____

YEAR: _____

_____

_____

_____

JANUARY 3

What is the most important thing
you learned today?

YEAR: _____

_____

_____

_____

YEAR: _____

_____

_____

_____

YEAR: _____

_____

_____

_____

JANUARY 4

If you could change something
about your day, what would it be?

YEAR: _____

_____

_____

_____

YEAR: _____

_____

_____

_____

YEAR: _____

_____

_____

_____

JANUARY 5

What is your favorite holiday?

YEAR: _____

_____

_____

YEAR: _____

_____

_____

YEAR: _____

_____

_____

JANUARY 6

If you were an animal, what
animal would you be?

YEAR: _____

_____

_____

_____

YEAR: _____

_____

_____

_____

YEAR: _____

_____

_____

_____

JANUARY 7

What is your favorite food?

YEAR: _____

_____

_____

YEAR: _____

_____

_____

YEAR: _____

_____

_____

JANUARY 8

Who is your best friend?

YEAR: _____

YEAR: _____

YEAR: _____

JANUARY 9

What is the best part of your
school day?

YEAR: _____

_____

_____

_____

YEAR: _____

_____

_____

_____

YEAR: _____

_____

_____

_____

JANUARY 10

When I woke up today, I felt

_____.

YEAR: _____

_____

_____

_____

YEAR: _____

_____

_____

_____

YEAR: _____

_____

_____

JANUARY 11

Who do you have lots of
love for today?

YEAR: _____

_____

_____

_____

YEAR: _____

_____

_____

_____

YEAR: _____

_____

_____

_____

JANUARY 12

What is the best news you've
heard lately?

YEAR: _____

_____

_____

_____

YEAR: _____

_____

_____

_____

YEAR: _____

_____

_____

_____

JANUARY 13

How do you feel about growing up?

YEAR: _____

_____

_____

_____

YEAR: _____

_____

_____

_____

YEAR: _____

_____

_____

_____

JANUARY 14

How happy are you today?

YEAR: _____

_____

_____

_____

YEAR: _____

_____

_____

_____

YEAR: _____

_____

_____

_____

JANUARY 15

What is the last dream
you remember?

YEAR: _____

_____

_____

_____

YEAR: _____

_____

_____

_____

YEAR: _____

_____

_____

_____

JANUARY 16

What famous person would you like to meet?

YEAR: _____

_____

_____

_____

YEAR: _____

_____

_____

_____

YEAR: _____

_____

_____

_____

JANUARY 17

Who in your life is most like you?

YEAR: _____

_____

_____

_____

YEAR: _____

_____

_____

_____

YEAR: _____

_____

_____

_____

JANUARY 18

What makes you nervous?

YEAR: _____

_____

_____

_____

YEAR: _____

_____

_____

_____

YEAR: _____

_____

_____

_____

JANUARY 19

How would you
describe your style?

YEAR: _____

_____

_____

_____

YEAR: _____

_____

_____

_____

YEAR: _____

_____

_____

_____

JANUARY 20

When was the last time you
were in big trouble?

YEAR: _____

_____

_____

_____

YEAR: _____

_____

_____

_____

YEAR: _____

_____

_____

_____

JANUARY 21

How do you think someone
would describe you?

YEAR: _____

YEAR: _____

YEAR: _____

JANUARY 22

What do you need to do today?

YEAR: _____

YEAR: _____

YEAR: _____

JANUARY 23

What do you want the
most right now?

YEAR: _____

_____

_____

_____

YEAR: _____

_____

_____

_____

YEAR: _____

_____

_____

_____

JANUARY 24

With whom would you want to
be stranded on a deserted island?

YEAR: 2024
My Brother and sister
and DaD, Mom.

YEAR:

YEAR:

JANUARY 25

Whom would you call
in an emergency?

YEAR: _____

_____

_____

_____

YEAR: _____

_____

_____

_____

YEAR: _____

_____

_____

_____

JANUARY 26

Whom have you talked to on the
phone most recently?

YEAR: _____

_____

_____

YEAR: _____

_____

_____

YEAR: _____

_____

_____

JANUARY 27

What is your favorite video game?

YEAR: _____

_____

_____

_____

YEAR: _____

_____

_____

_____

YEAR: _____

_____

_____

_____

JANUARY 28

What is your usual breakfast?

YEAR: _____

_____

_____

_____

YEAR: _____

_____

_____

_____

YEAR: _____

_____

_____

_____

JANUARY 29

What is your favorite season?

YEAR: _____

_____

_____

_____

YEAR: _____

_____

_____

_____

YEAR: _____

_____

_____

_____

JANUARY 30

What is your favorite app?

YEAR: _____

_____

_____

_____

YEAR: _____

_____

_____

_____

YEAR: _____

_____

_____

_____

JANUARY 31

If you had to move, where would
you want to go?

YEAR: _____

YEAR: _____

YEAR: _____

FEBRUARY 1

What is the best book
you've read lately?

YEAR: _____

YEAR: _____

YEAR: _____

FEBRUARY 2

What store is your favorite?

YEAR: _____

_____

_____

YEAR: _____

_____

_____

_____

YEAR: _____

_____

_____

_____

FEBRUARY 3

What type of candy do you like best?

YEAR: _____

_____
_____
_____

YEAR: _____

_____
_____
_____

YEAR: _____

_____
_____
_____

FEBRUARY 4

What is your favorite
sport to play?

YEAR: _____

_____

_____

_____

YEAR: _____

_____

_____

_____

YEAR: _____

_____

_____

_____

FEBRUARY 5

Who is your favorite teacher?

YEAR: _____

_____

_____

_____

YEAR: _____

_____

_____

_____

YEAR: _____

_____

_____

_____

FEBRUARY 6

What is your favorite thing
about your home?

YEAR: _____

_____

_____

_____

YEAR: _____

_____

_____

_____

YEAR: _____

_____

_____

_____

FEBRUARY 7

If you could do anything today,
what would you do?

YEAR: _____

_____

_____

_____

YEAR: _____

_____

_____

_____

YEAR: _____

_____

_____

_____

FEBRUARY 8

How much homework did you do this week?

YEAR: _____

_____

_____

_____

YEAR: _____

_____

_____

_____

YEAR: _____

_____

_____

_____

FEBRUARY 9

What is your favorite
thing about yourself?

YEAR: _____

YEAR: _____

YEAR: _____

FEBRUARY 10

What gift have you received lately?

YEAR: _____

_____

_____

YEAR: _____

_____

_____

YEAR: _____

_____

_____

FEBRUARY 11

Whom would you invite
if you had a party?

YEAR: _____

_____

_____

_____

YEAR: _____

_____

_____

_____

YEAR: _____

_____

_____

_____

FEBRUARY 12

How do you feel about
arts and crafts?

YEAR: _____

_____

_____

YEAR: _____

_____

_____

_____

YEAR: _____

_____

_____

_____

FEBRUARY 13

What would you like
to be able to cook?

YEAR: _____

YEAR: _____

YEAR: _____

FEBRUARY 14

Who is your Valentine?

YEAR: _____

_____

_____

_____

YEAR: _____

_____

_____

_____

YEAR: _____

_____

_____

_____

FEBRUARY 15

Who loves you?

YEAR: _____

_____

_____

_____

YEAR: _____

_____

_____

_____

YEAR: _____

_____

_____

_____

FEBRUARY 16

Whom do you trust with
your secrets?

YEAR: _____

_____

_____

_____

YEAR: _____

_____

_____

_____

YEAR: _____

_____

_____

_____

FEBRUARY 17

What was the best thing that
happened to you today?

YEAR: _____

_____

_____

YEAR: _____

_____

_____

YEAR: _____

_____

_____

FEBRUARY 18

Have you told a lie recently?

YEAR: _____

_____

_____

YEAR: _____

_____

_____

_____

YEAR: _____

_____

_____

_____

FEBRUARY 19

What is your favorite joke?

YEAR: _____

_____

_____

_____

YEAR: _____

_____

_____

_____

YEAR: _____

_____

_____

_____

FEBRUARY 20

What is your favorite possession?

YEAR: _____

_____

_____

_____

YEAR: _____

_____

_____

_____

YEAR: _____

_____

_____

_____

FEBRUARY 21

Who really understands you?

YEAR: _____

_____

_____

YEAR: _____

_____

_____

YEAR: _____

_____

_____

FEBRUARY 22

What would you never give away?

YEAR: _____

_____

_____

_____

YEAR: _____

_____

_____

_____

YEAR: _____

_____

_____

_____

FEBRUARY 23

What is your favorite song?

YEAR: _____

_____

_____

YEAR: _____

_____

_____

YEAR: _____

_____

_____

FEBRUARY 24

Who is your favorite
professional sports player?

YEAR: _____

_____

_____

YEAR: _____

_____

_____

_____

YEAR: _____

_____

_____

_____

FEBRUARY 25

What do you worry about?

YEAR: _____

_____

_____

_____

YEAR: _____

_____

_____

_____

YEAR: _____

_____

_____

_____

FEBRUARY 26

What are you excited about?

YEAR: _____

_____

_____

_____

YEAR: _____

_____

_____

_____

YEAR: _____

_____

_____

_____

FEBRUARY 27

What memory makes you smile?

YEAR: _____

_____

_____

_____

YEAR: _____

_____

_____

_____

YEAR: _____

_____

_____

_____

FEBRUARY 28

If you could change your name,
what would you change it to?

YEAR: _____

YEAR: _____

YEAR: _____

FEBRUARY 29

What did you last cry about?

YEAR: _____

_____

_____

_____

YEAR: _____

_____

_____

_____

YEAR: _____

_____

_____

_____

MARCH 1

What wild animal would you
keep as a pet if you could?

YEAR: _____

_____

_____

_____

YEAR: _____

_____

_____

_____

YEAR: _____

_____

_____

_____

MARCH 2

What do you think
about a lot lately?

YEAR: _____

YEAR: _____

YEAR: _____

MARCH 3

How do you get to school?

YEAR: _____

_____

_____

_____

YEAR: _____

_____

_____

_____

YEAR: _____

_____

_____

_____

MARCH 4

If you could write a book,
what would it be about?

YEAR: _____

_____

_____

_____

YEAR: _____

_____

_____

_____

YEAR: _____

_____

_____

_____

MARCH 5

If you could eat one food all day
long, what would it be?

YEAR: _____

_____

_____

_____

YEAR: _____

_____

_____

_____

YEAR: _____

_____

_____

_____

MARCH 6

When was the last time
you were sick?

YEAR: _____

_____

_____

_____

YEAR: _____

_____

_____

_____

YEAR: _____

_____

_____

_____

MARCH 7

Describe your day in one word.

YEAR: _____

_____

_____

_____

YEAR: _____

_____

_____

_____

YEAR: _____

_____

_____

_____

MARCH 8

One person whom I don't really
trust is _____ .

YEAR: _____

YEAR: _____

YEAR: _____

MARCH 9

The funniest person I know is

_____.

YEAR: _____

_____

_____

_____

YEAR: _____

_____

_____

_____

YEAR: _____

_____

_____

_____

MARCH 10

What is your favorite
kind of weather?

YEAR: _____

_____
_____
_____

YEAR: _____

_____
_____
_____

YEAR: _____

_____
_____
_____

MARCH 11

What do you like taking care of?

YEAR: _____

_____

_____

_____

YEAR: _____

_____

_____

_____

YEAR: _____

_____

_____

_____

MARCH 12

Would you want to live forever?

YEAR: _____

_____

_____

_____

YEAR: _____

_____

_____

_____

YEAR: _____

_____

_____

_____

MARCH 13

Where was your last vacation?

YEAR: _____

_____

_____

_____

YEAR: _____

_____

_____

_____

YEAR: _____

_____

_____

_____

MARCH 14

What did you do today?

YEAR: _____

_____

_____

_____

YEAR: _____

_____

_____

_____

YEAR: _____

_____

_____

_____

MARCH 15

Whose mind do you wish
you could read?

YEAR: _____

_____

_____

_____

YEAR: _____

_____

_____

_____

YEAR: _____

_____

_____

_____

MARCH 16

Whom do you want to be most like?

YEAR: _____

_____

_____

_____

YEAR: _____

_____

_____

_____

YEAR: _____

_____

_____

_____

MARCH 17

What's the best advice that
you have received?

YEAR: _____

_____

_____

_____

YEAR: _____

_____

_____

_____

YEAR: _____

_____

_____

_____

MARCH 18

What is one promise
you have made?

YEAR: _____

_____

_____

_____

YEAR: _____

_____

_____

_____

YEAR: _____

_____

_____

_____

MARCH 19

What do you like most
about your mom or dad?

YEAR: _____

_____

_____

_____

YEAR: _____

_____

_____

_____

YEAR: _____

_____

_____

_____

MARCH 20

What's the last thing
you made by hand?

YEAR: _____

_____

_____

_____

YEAR: _____

_____

_____

_____

YEAR: _____

_____

_____

_____

MARCH 21

In the spring, I like to

_____.

YEAR: _____

_____

_____

_____

YEAR: _____

_____

_____

_____

YEAR: _____

_____

_____

_____

MARCH 22

Do you believe dreams come true?

YEAR: _____

_____

_____

YEAR: _____

_____

_____

YEAR: _____

_____

_____

MARCH 23

What act of kindness
could you offer today?

YEAR: _____

_____

_____

_____

YEAR: _____

_____

_____

_____

YEAR: _____

_____

_____

_____

MARCH 24

What was the last thing you had
a nightmare about?

YEAR: _____

_____

_____

YEAR: _____

_____

_____

YEAR: _____

_____

_____

MARCH 25

What is the last thing you read?

YEAR: _____

_____

_____

YEAR: _____

_____

_____

YEAR: _____

_____

_____

MARCH 26

What would you like
to change in the world?

YEAR: _____

YEAR: _____

YEAR: _____

MARCH 27

How do you feel today?

YEAR: _____

_____

_____

_____

YEAR: _____

_____

_____

_____

YEAR: _____

_____

_____

_____

MARCH 28

What makes you jump for joy?

YEAR: _____

_____

_____

_____

YEAR: _____

_____

_____

_____

YEAR: _____

_____

_____

_____

MARCH 29

Describe the last time you were mad
at your mom/dad/brother/sister.

YEAR:

YEAR:

YEAR:

MARCH 30

Who is the most important
person in your life?

YEAR: _____

YEAR: _____

YEAR: _____

MARCH 31

What have you
accomplished today?

YEAR: _____ _

_____

_____

_____

YEAR: _____

_____

_____

_____

YEAR: _____

_____

_____

_____

APRIL 1

Describe your dream house.

YEAR: _____

_____

_____

_____

YEAR: _____

_____

_____

_____

YEAR: _____

_____

_____

_____

APRIL 2

What is your favorite
school memory?

YEAR: _____

_____

_____

_____

YEAR: _____

_____

_____

_____

YEAR: _____

_____

_____

_____

APRIL 3

Describe the perfect day.

YEAR: _____

_____

_____

_____

YEAR: _____

_____

_____

_____

YEAR: _____

_____

_____

_____

APRIL 4

I have never been more scared
than when _____.

YEAR: _____

_____

_____

YEAR: _____

_____

_____

YEAR: _____

_____

_____

APRIL 5

Five years from now, I will be

_____.

YEAR: _____

_____

_____

_____

YEAR: _____

_____

_____

_____

YEAR: _____

_____

_____

_____

APRIL 6

One person I need a break from

is _____.

YEAR: _____

YEAR: _____

YEAR: _____

APRIL 7

I will never _____.

YEAR: _____

_____

_____

_____

YEAR: _____

_____

_____

_____

YEAR: _____

_____

_____

_____

APRIL 8

What did you enjoy most about today?

YEAR: _____

_____

_____

_____

YEAR: _____

_____

_____

_____

YEAR: _____

_____

_____

_____

APRIL 9

Who is the last person who
told you they love you?

YEAR: _____

_____

_____

_____

YEAR: _____

_____

_____

_____

YEAR: _____

_____

_____

_____

APRIL 10

What is the toughest challenge
you have faced lately?

YEAR: _____

_____

_____

_____

YEAR: _____

_____

_____

_____

YEAR: _____

_____

_____

_____

APRIL 11

Your house is "home" because

_____.

YEAR: _____

_____

_____

_____

YEAR: _____

_____

_____

_____

YEAR: _____

_____

_____

_____

APRIL 12

Today, the temperature was

_____ .

YEAR: _____

_____

_____

YEAR: _____

_____

_____

YEAR: _____

_____

_____

APRIL 13

What is something you
want to improve at?

YEAR: _____

_____

_____

_____

YEAR: _____

_____

_____

_____

YEAR: _____

_____

_____

_____

APRIL 14

What mistake have
you made lately?

YEAR:

YEAR:

YEAR:

APRIL 15

Whom or what are you
thankful for today?

YEAR: _____

_____

_____

_____

YEAR: _____

_____

_____

_____

YEAR: _____

_____

_____

_____

APRIL 16

What is something you say a lot?

YEAR: _____

_____

_____

_____

YEAR: _____

_____

_____

_____

YEAR: _____

_____

_____

_____

APRIL 17

What song makes
you want to dance?

YEAR: _____

_____

_____

_____

YEAR: _____

_____

_____

_____

YEAR: _____

_____

_____

_____

APRIL 18

What is your dream birthday party?

YEAR: _____

_____

_____

YEAR: _____

_____

_____

YEAR: _____

_____

_____

APRIL 19

What is your favorite
thing to draw?

YEAR: _____

YEAR: _____

YEAR: _____

APRIL 20

My hero is _____.

YEAR: _____

YEAR: _____

YEAR: _____

APRIL 21

Three things that make me
happy are _____.

YEAR: _____

_____

_____

_____

YEAR: _____

_____

_____

_____

YEAR: _____

_____

_____

_____

APRIL 22

My family embarrasses me
when they _____.

YEAR: _____

_____

_____

_____

YEAR: _____

_____

_____

_____

YEAR: _____

_____

_____

_____

APRIL 23

When speaking in front of my
class, I feel _____.

YEAR: _____

_____
_____

YEAR: _____

_____
_____
_____

YEAR: _____

_____
_____

APRIL 24

My favorite thing to do on rainy
days is _____.

YEAR: _____

_____

_____

YEAR: _____

_____

_____

YEAR: _____

_____

_____

APRIL 25

Would you rather sleep late
or get up early?

YEAR: _____

YEAR: _____

YEAR: _____

APRIL 26

What are your unique qualities?

YEAR: _____

YEAR: _____

YEAR: _____

APRIL 27

What makes you feel
comfy and cozy?

YEAR: _____

_____

_____

_____

YEAR: _____

_____

_____

_____

YEAR: _____

_____

_____

_____

APRIL 28

What is your favorite cereal?

YEAR: _____

_____

_____

_____

YEAR: _____

_____

_____

_____

YEAR: _____

_____

_____

_____

APRIL 29

What would be the
worst job to have?

YEAR: _____

_____

_____

_____

YEAR: _____

_____

_____

_____

YEAR: _____

_____

_____

_____

APRIL 30

What is the most
valuable thing you own?

YEAR: _____

_____

_____

_____

YEAR: _____

_____

_____

_____

YEAR: _____

_____

_____

_____

MAY 1

What is the last grade you received,
and how did you feel about it?

YEAR: _____

YEAR: _____

YEAR: _____

MAY 2

Who is your favorite artist?

YEAR: _____

_____

_____

_____

YEAR: _____

_____

_____

_____

YEAR: _____

_____

_____

_____

MAY 3

What is one of your talents?

YEAR:

YEAR:

YEAR:

MAY 4

Who got in trouble at school lately?

YEAR: _____

_____

_____

_____

YEAR: _____

_____

_____

_____

YEAR: _____

_____

_____

_____

MAY 5

What three television shows do
you watch the most?

YEAR: _____

_____

_____

YEAR: _____

_____

_____

_____

YEAR: _____

_____

_____

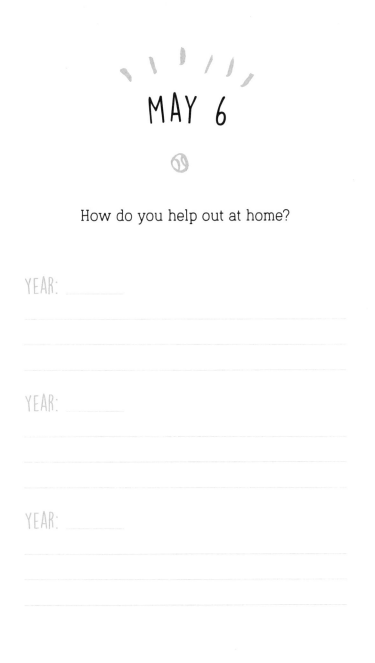

MAY 6

How do you help out at home?

YEAR: _____

YEAR: _____

YEAR: _____

MAY 7

My family is wonderful because

——————————— .

YEAR: _____

_____

_____

_____

YEAR: _____

_____

_____

_____

YEAR: _____

_____

_____

_____

MAY 8

If I could buy anything I wanted,
I would buy _____.

YEAR: _____

_____

_____

_____

YEAR: _____

_____

_____

_____

YEAR: _____

_____

_____

_____

MAY 9

I like teaching others how to

_____ .

YEAR: _____

YEAR: _____

YEAR: _____

MAY 10

What do your parents nag you about sometimes?

YEAR: _____

YEAR: _____

YEAR: _____

MAY 11

On a scale of 1-10, how likely
are you to take a risk?

YEAR: _____

YEAR: _____

YEAR: _____

MAY 12

What favor has someone
done for you lately?

YEAR:

YEAR:

YEAR:

MAY 13

How much time do you
spend on social media?

YEAR: _____

_____

_____

YEAR: _____

_____

_____

YEAR: _____

_____

_____

MAY 14

What makes you *you*?

YEAR:

YEAR:

YEAR:

MAY 15

Whom do you have trouble
getting along with?

YEAR: _____

_____

_____

_____

YEAR: _____

_____

_____

_____

YEAR: _____

_____

_____

_____

MAY 16

I am awesome at

_____ .

YEAR: _____

_____

_____

_____

YEAR: _____

_____

_____

_____

YEAR: _____

_____

_____

_____

MAY 17

What do you collect?

YEAR: _____

_____

_____

_____

YEAR: _____

_____

_____

_____

YEAR: _____

_____

_____

_____

MAY 18

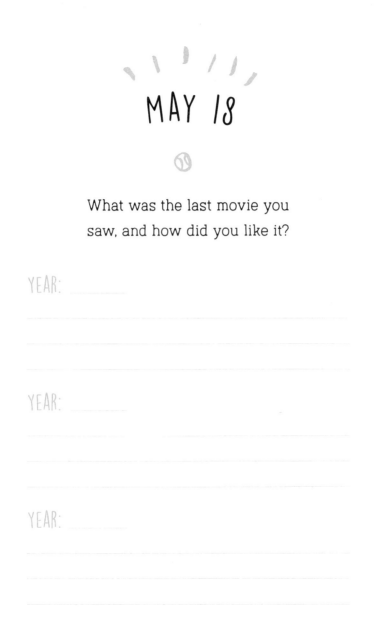

What was the last movie you
saw, and how did you like it?

YEAR:

YEAR:

YEAR:

MAY 19

What concert would you
love to get tickets for?

YEAR: _____

_____

_____

_____

YEAR: _____

_____

_____

_____

YEAR: _____

_____

_____

_____

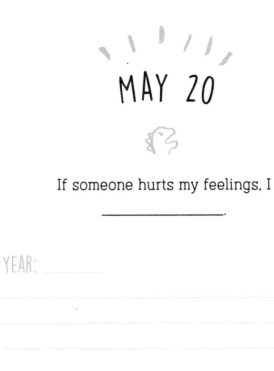

MAY 20

If someone hurts my feelings, I
_____.

YEAR: _____

_____

_____

_____

YEAR: _____

_____

_____

_____

YEAR: _____

_____

_____

_____

MAY 21

What do you like
doing on your own?

YEAR: _____

_____

_____

_____

YEAR: _____

_____

_____

_____

YEAR: _____

_____

_____

_____

MAY 22

I have never _____.

YEAR: _____

_____

_____

_____

YEAR: _____

_____

_____

_____

YEAR: _____

_____

_____

_____

MAY 23

I wish I loved

_____ more.

YEAR: _____

YEAR: _____

YEAR: _____

MAY 24

Who is your favorite grown-up?

YEAR: _____

_____

_____

_____

YEAR: _____

_____

_____

_____

YEAR: _____

_____

_____

_____

MAY 25

What good habits do you have?

YEAR: _____

_____

_____

_____

YEAR: _____

_____

_____

_____

YEAR: _____

_____

_____

_____

MAY 26

I think the world is a

_____ place.

MAY 27

I wish my parents would let me

_____ .

YEAR: _____

_____

_____

YEAR: _____

_____

_____

YEAR: _____

_____

_____

MAY 28

One thing I love about my school
is _____.

YEAR: _____

_____

_____

_____

YEAR: _____

_____

_____

_____

YEAR: _____

_____

_____

_____

MAY 29

I don't eat _____ .

YEAR: _____

_____

_____

_____

YEAR: _____

_____

_____

_____

YEAR: _____

_____

_____

_____

MAY 30

If you could change one rule in
your house, what would it be?

YEAR: _____

YEAR: _____

YEAR: _____

MAY 31

What kind of friend are you?

YEAR: _____

_____

_____

_____

YEAR: _____

_____

_____

_____

YEAR: _____

_____

_____

_____

JUNE 1

What is your favorite word?

YEAR: _____

YEAR: _____

YEAR: _____

JUNE 2

What did you do for your
most recent birthday?

YEAR: _____

_____

_____

_____

YEAR: _____

_____

_____

_____

YEAR: _____

_____

_____

_____

JUNE 3

How do you spend recess time?

YEAR: _____

YEAR: _____

YEAR: _____

Birthday

JUNE 4

When is the last time
you won something?*

YEAR: _____

_____

_____

_____

YEAR: _____

_____

_____

_____

YEAR: _____

_____

_____

_____

JUNE 5

List four things that are
important to you right now.

JUNE 6

How organized are you?

YEAR: _____

_____

_____

_____

YEAR: _____

_____

_____

_____

YEAR: _____

_____

_____

_____

JUNE 7

How would your friends
describe you?

YEAR: _____

_____

_____

_____

YEAR: _____

_____

_____

_____

YEAR: _____

_____

_____

_____

JUNE 8

How do you cheer up your friends?

YEAR: _____

_____

_____

_____

YEAR: _____

_____

_____

_____

YEAR: _____

_____

_____

_____

JUNE 9

Who is your weirdest friend
or family member?

YEAR: _____

_____

_____

_____

YEAR: _____

_____

_____

_____

YEAR: _____

_____

_____

_____

JUNE 10

If all your clothes had to be one
color, what color would you choose?

YEAR: _____

_____

_____

_____

YEAR: _____

_____

_____

_____

YEAR: _____

_____

_____

_____

JUNE 11

If you could pick a classmate to run your
school, whom would it be and why?

YEAR: _____

_____

_____

YEAR: _____

_____

_____

YEAR: _____

_____

_____

JUNE 12

On what do you spend
most of your money?

YEAR: _____

_____

_____

YEAR: _____

_____

_____

YEAR: _____

_____

_____

JUNE 13

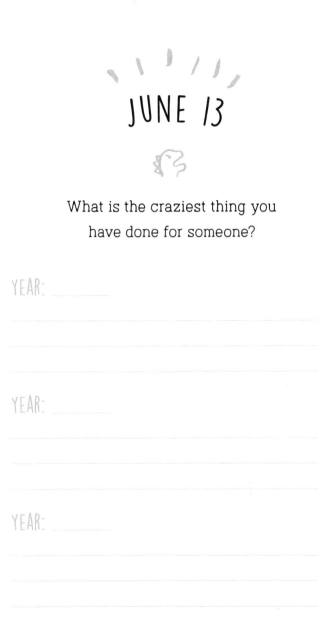

What is the craziest thing you
have done for someone?

YEAR:

YEAR:

YEAR:

JUNE 14

What was your last adventure?

YEAR: _____

_____

_____

_____

YEAR: _____

_____

_____

_____

YEAR: _____

_____

_____

_____

JUNE 15

I am too old to _____.

YEAR: _____

_____

_____

_____

YEAR: _____

_____

_____

_____

YEAR: _____

_____

_____

_____

JUNE 16

What is the grossest thing
you've ever seen?

YEAR: _____

YEAR: _____

YEAR: _____

JUNE 17

I hope I don't _____

when I am older.

YEAR: _____

_____

_____

_____

YEAR: _____

_____

_____

_____

YEAR: _____

_____

_____

_____

JUNE 18

What advice would you give
to younger kids?

YEAR: _____

_____

_____

YEAR: _____

_____

_____

_____

YEAR: _____

_____

_____

_____

JUNE 19

Who has the best hair?

YEAR: _____

_____

_____

_____

YEAR: _____

_____

_____

_____

YEAR: _____

_____

_____

_____

JUNE 20

I wish I had the courage to

_____ .

YEAR: _____

_____

_____

_____

YEAR: _____

_____

_____

_____

YEAR: _____

_____

_____

_____

JUNE 21

My favorite school lunch is

_____ .

YEAR: _____

_____

_____

YEAR: _____

_____

_____

_____

YEAR: _____

_____

_____

_____

JUNE 22

When I am with my friends, we
like to _____.

YEAR: _____

_____

_____

_____

YEAR: _____

_____

_____

_____

YEAR: _____

_____

_____

_____

JUNE 23

The longest I have been away
from home is _____ .

YEAR: _____

_____

_____

YEAR: _____

_____

_____

_____

YEAR: _____

_____

_____

_____

JUNE 24

What are you focused on today?

YEAR: _____

_____

_____

_____

YEAR: _____

_____

_____

_____

YEAR: _____

_____

_____

_____

JUNE 25

If I could get any kind of dog, I
would get a _____.

YEAR: _____

_____

_____

_____

YEAR: _____

_____

_____

_____

YEAR: _____

_____

_____

_____

JUNE 26

What new food have you tried,
and did you like it?

YEAR: _____

_____

_____

YEAR: _____

_____

_____

YEAR: _____

_____

_____

JUNE 27

What did you love last year
that you hate this year?

YEAR: _____

_____

_____

_____

YEAR: _____

_____

_____

_____

YEAR: _____

_____

_____

_____

JUNE 28

I get embarrassed when

_____ .

YEAR: _____

_____

_____

_____

YEAR: _____

_____

_____

_____

YEAR: _____

_____

_____

_____

JUNE 29

If you could grow up to be famous,
what would you be famous for?

YEAR: _____

_____

_____

_____

YEAR: _____

_____

_____

_____

YEAR: _____

_____

_____

_____

JUNE 30

What is the hardest thing
about being a kid?

YEAR: _____

_____

_____

_____

YEAR: _____

_____

_____

_____

YEAR: _____

_____

_____

_____

JULY 1

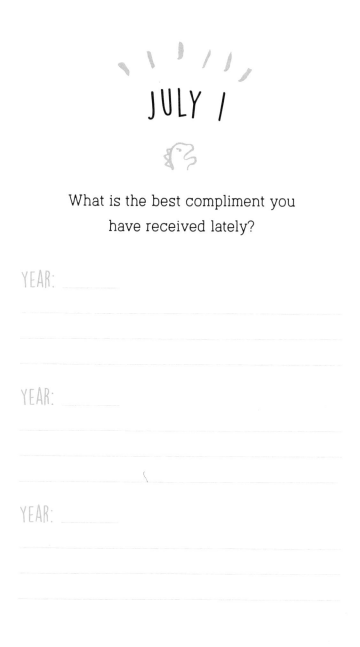

What is the best compliment you
have received lately?

YEAR: _____

_____

_____

YEAR: _____

_____

_____

YEAR: _____

_____

_____

JULY 2

What is your favorite
pizza topping?

YEAR: _____

_____

_____

_____

YEAR: _____

_____

_____

_____

YEAR: _____

_____

_____

_____

JULY 3

Have you ever lied to someone
close to you? If so, about what?

YEAR:

YEAR:

YEAR:

JULY 4

If you could invent something to
make life easier, what would it be?

YEAR: _____

YEAR: _____

YEAR: _____

JULY 5

When was a time
that you felt lucky?

YEAR: _____

YEAR: _____

YEAR: _____

JULY 6

If you could make one rule that everyone
had to follow, what would it be?

YEAR: _____

_____

_____

_____

YEAR: _____

_____

_____

_____

YEAR: _____

_____

_____

_____

JULY 7

What do you enjoy doing
with your family?

YEAR: _____

_____

_____

_____

YEAR: _____

_____

_____

_____

YEAR: _____

_____

_____

_____

JULY 8

When you grow up, do you want
to have kids? If so, how many?

YEAR: _____

YEAR: _____

YEAR: _____

JULY 9

Did anyone push
your buttons today?

YEAR: _____

_____

_____

_____

YEAR: _____

_____

_____

_____

YEAR: _____

_____

_____

_____

JULY 10

Whom would you like to
be friends with?

YEAR: _____

_____

_____

_____

YEAR: _____

_____

_____

_____

YEAR: _____

_____

_____

_____

JULY 11

What was the toughest
part of your day?

YEAR: _____

_____

_____

_____

YEAR: _____

_____

_____

_____

YEAR: _____

_____

_____

_____

JULY 12

If you won a hundred dollars,
what would you buy?

YEAR: _____

_____

_____

_____

YEAR: _____

_____

_____

_____

YEAR: _____

_____

_____

_____

JULY 13

When you are bored,
what do you tend to do?

YEAR: _____

_____

_____

_____

YEAR: _____

_____

_____

_____

YEAR: _____

_____

_____

_____

JULY 14

What is your favorite
smell, and why?

YEAR: _____

_____

_____

_____

YEAR: _____

_____

_____

_____

YEAR: _____

_____

_____

_____

JULY 15

If you could have dinner with
anyone, who would it be?

YEAR: _____

_____

_____

_____

YEAR: _____

_____

_____

_____

YEAR: _____

_____

_____

_____

JULY 16

If you could have a superpower,
what would it be?

YEAR: _____

_____

_____

_____

YEAR: _____

_____

_____

_____

YEAR: _____

_____

_____

_____

JULY 17

What is something you want
to learn how to do?

YEAR: _____

_____

_____

_____

YEAR: _____

_____

_____

_____

YEAR: _____

_____

_____

_____

JULY 18

What should you do more often?

YEAR: _____

_____

_____

_____

YEAR: _____

_____

_____

_____

YEAR: _____

_____

_____

_____

JULY 19

If you were granted one wish,
what would it be?

YEAR: _____

_____

_____

_____

YEAR: _____

_____

_____

_____

YEAR: _____

_____

_____

_____

JULY 20

What are three qualities
that make a good friend?

YEAR: _____

_____

_____

_____

YEAR: _____

_____

_____

_____

YEAR: _____

_____

_____

_____

JULY 21

When I have a problem, I turn to

_____ .

YEAR: _____

_____

_____

_____

YEAR: _____

_____

_____

_____

YEAR: _____

_____

_____

_____

JULY 22

What is in the bottom of your
backpack right now?

YEAR: _____

_____

_____

_____

YEAR: _____

_____

_____

_____

YEAR: _____

_____

_____

_____

JULY 23

The nicest thing my parents have done for (or said to) me is _____.

YEAR: _____

_____

_____

_____

YEAR: _____

_____

_____

_____

YEAR: _____

_____

_____

_____

JULY 24

How do you earn money?

YEAR: _____

_____

_____

_____

YEAR: _____

_____

_____

_____

YEAR: _____

_____

_____

_____

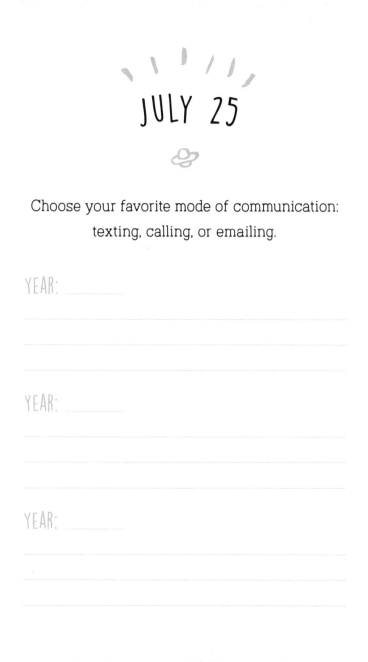

JULY 25

Choose your favorite mode of communication:
texting, calling, or emailing.

YEAR: _____

_____

_____

YEAR: _____

_____

_____

YEAR: _____

_____

_____

JULY 26

Before I go to sleep, I like to

_____.

YEAR: _____

_____

_____

_____

YEAR: _____

_____

_____

_____

YEAR: _____

_____

_____

_____

JULY 27

I could talk for hours about

_____.

YEAR: _____

_____

_____

_____

YEAR: _____

_____

_____

_____

YEAR: _____

_____

_____

_____

JULY 28

The chore I hate most is

_____.

YEAR: _____

_____

_____

_____

YEAR: _____

_____

_____

_____

YEAR: _____

_____

_____

_____

JULY 29

I think my teacher would say
that I'm _____.

YEAR: _____

_____

_____

_____

YEAR: _____

_____

_____

_____

YEAR: _____

_____

_____

_____

JULY 30

Who is your favorite fiction character?

YEAR: _____

_____

_____

_____

YEAR: _____

_____

_____

_____

YEAR: _____

_____

_____

_____

JULY 31

If you could change one thing about
your best friend, what would it be?

YEAR: _____

_____

_____

_____

YEAR: _____

_____

_____

_____

YEAR: _____

_____

_____

_____

AUGUST 1

How do you feel about the
upcoming school year?

YEAR: _____

_____

_____

_____

YEAR: _____

_____

_____

_____

YEAR: _____

_____

_____

_____

AUGUST 2

Where do you go to be alone?

YEAR: _____

_____

_____

_____

YEAR: _____

_____

_____

_____

YEAR: _____

_____

_____

_____

AUGUST 3

If you could be a character in a show,
which character would you be?

YEAR: _____

_____

_____

_____

YEAR: _____

_____

_____

_____

YEAR: _____

_____

_____

_____

AUGUST 4

What is the best place on Earth?

YEAR: _____

_____

_____

_____

YEAR: _____

_____

_____

_____

YEAR: _____

_____

_____

_____

AUGUST 5

What is one habit you'd like to break?

YEAR: _____

_____

_____

_____

YEAR: _____

_____

_____

_____

YEAR: _____

_____

_____

_____

AUGUST 6

I think I'd be amazing at

_____.

YEAR: _____

_____

_____

_____

YEAR: _____

_____

_____

_____

YEAR: _____

_____

_____

_____

AUGUST 7

What makes you uncomfortable?

YEAR: _____

_____

_____

_____

YEAR: _____

_____

_____

_____

YEAR: _____

_____

_____

_____

AUGUST 8

What would you change
at your school?

YEAR: _____

_____

_____

_____

YEAR: _____

_____

_____

_____

YEAR: _____

_____

_____

_____

AUGUST 9

Since I started doing
_____,I feel better.

YEAR: _____

_____

_____

YEAR: _____

_____

_____

YEAR: _____

_____

_____

AUGUST 10

I care about the environment
because _____.

YEAR: _____

YEAR: _____

YEAR: _____

AUGUST 11

Of all the things you've learned, what do you think will be the most useful as an adult?

YEAR: _____

_____

_____

_____

YEAR: _____

_____

_____

_____

YEAR: _____

_____

_____

_____

AUGUST 12

What question do you wish you
could ask someone?

YEAR: _____

_____

_____

_____

YEAR: _____

_____

_____

_____

YEAR: _____

_____

_____

_____

AUGUST 13

What makes your parents
proud of you?

YEAR: _____

_____

_____

_____

YEAR: _____

_____

_____

_____

YEAR: _____

_____

_____

_____

AUGUST 14

If you could design a shirt, what word, saying, or picture would you print on it?

YEAR: _____

_____

_____

_____

YEAR: _____

_____

_____

_____

YEAR: _____

_____

_____

_____

AUGUST 15

What private joke do you
share with a friend?

YEAR: _____

_____

_____

_____

YEAR: _____

_____

_____

_____

YEAR: _____

_____

_____

_____

AUGUST 16

What is your favorite thing about
your bedroom?

YEAR: _____

_____

_____

_____

YEAR: _____

_____

_____

_____

YEAR: _____

_____

_____

_____

AUGUST 17

What is your favorite
thing about your town?

YEAR: _____

_____

_____

_____

YEAR: _____

_____

_____

_____

YEAR: _____

_____

_____

_____

AUGUST 18

If you could drive somewhere
today, where would you go?

YEAR: _____

_____

_____

_____

YEAR: _____

_____

_____

_____

YEAR: _____

_____

_____

_____

AUGUST 19

What is your favorite restaurant?

YEAR: _____

_____

_____

_____

YEAR: _____

_____

_____

_____

YEAR: _____

_____

_____

_____

AUGUST 20

What do you regret saying?

YEAR: _____

_____

_____

_____

YEAR: _____

_____

_____

_____

YEAR: _____

_____

_____

_____

AUGUST 21

How close are you to your grandparent(s)?

YEAR: _____

_____

_____

_____

YEAR: _____

_____

_____

_____

YEAR: _____

_____

_____

_____

AUGUST 22

What is your favorite
summer activity?

YEAR: _____

YEAR: _____

YEAR: _____

AUGUST 23

What is your favorite
flavor of ice cream?

YEAR: _____

_____

_____

_____

YEAR: _____

_____

_____

_____

YEAR: _____

_____

_____

_____

AUGUST 24

Who do you count on the most?

YEAR: _____

_____

_____

_____

YEAR: _____

_____

_____

_____

YEAR: _____

_____

_____

_____

AUGUST 25

Which friend do you think
you'll have forever?

YEAR: _____

_____

_____

_____

YEAR: _____

_____

_____

_____

YEAR: _____

_____

_____

_____

AUGUST 26

If your life was a novel, what
would the title be?

YEAR: _____

_____

_____

_____

YEAR: _____

_____

_____

_____

YEAR: _____

_____

_____

_____

AUGUST 27

Where do you want to live
when you grow up?

YEAR: _____

_____

_____

YEAR: _____

_____

_____

YEAR: _____

_____

_____

AUGUST 28

What board game or video game
are you best at?

YEAR: _____

_____

_____

_____

YEAR: _____

_____

_____

_____

YEAR: _____

_____

_____

_____

AUGUST 29

What class do you dread?

YEAR: _____

_____

_____

_____

YEAR: _____

_____

_____

_____

YEAR: _____

_____

_____

_____

AUGUST 30

What foreign language would
you like to speak?

YEAR: _____

_____

_____

_____

YEAR: _____

_____

_____

_____

YEAR: _____

_____

_____

_____

AUGUST 31

What is your favorite dessert?

YEAR: _____

_____

_____

_____

YEAR: _____

_____

_____

_____

YEAR: _____

_____

_____

_____

SEPTEMBER /

What are you most proud of?

YEAR: _____

_____

_____

_____

YEAR: _____

_____

_____

_____

YEAR: _____

_____

_____

_____

SEPTEMBER 2

What is your favorite outfit?

YEAR: _____

_____

_____

_____

YEAR: _____

_____

_____

_____

YEAR: _____

_____

_____

_____

SEPTEMBER 3

What can't you sleep without?

YEAR: _____

_____

_____

_____

YEAR: _____

_____

_____

_____

YEAR: _____

_____

_____

_____

SEPTEMBER 4

If you could fly somewhere
today, where would you go?

YEAR: _____

_____

_____

_____

YEAR: _____

_____

_____

_____

YEAR: _____

_____

_____

_____

SEPTEMBER 5

Who is the first person you
thought of today?

YEAR: _____

_____

_____

_____

YEAR: _____

_____

_____

_____

YEAR: _____

_____

_____

_____

SEPTEMBER 6

Who was kind to you today?

YEAR: _____

YEAR: _____

YEAR: _____

SEPTEMBER 7

What was the worst thing that
happened to you today?

YEAR: _____

_____

_____

YEAR: _____

_____

_____

YEAR: _____

_____

_____

SEPTEMBER 8

What is your favorite
day of the week?

YEAR: _____

_____

_____

_____

YEAR: _____

_____

_____

_____

YEAR: _____

_____

_____

_____

SEPTEMBER 9

What do you see
outside your window?

YEAR: _____

_____

_____

_____

YEAR: _____

_____

_____

_____

YEAR: _____

_____

_____

_____

SEPTEMBER 10

If you could be any celebrity,
whom would you be?

YEAR: _____

_____

_____

_____

YEAR: _____

_____

_____

_____

YEAR: _____

_____

_____

_____

SEPTEMBER 11

What is the first thing
you did this morning?

YEAR:

YEAR:

YEAR:

SEPTEMBER 12

What was beautiful about today?

YEAR: _____

_____

_____

YEAR: _____

_____

_____

YEAR: _____

_____

_____

SEPTEMBER 13

Who is your biggest supporter?

YEAR: _____

_____

_____

_____

YEAR: _____

_____

_____

_____

YEAR: _____

_____

_____

_____

SEPTEMBER 14

What is your favorite movie?

YEAR: _____

_____

_____

_____

YEAR: _____

_____

_____

_____

YEAR: _____

_____

_____

_____

SEPTEMBER 15

What TV show makes you laugh?

YEAR: _____

_____

_____

_____

YEAR: _____

_____

_____

_____

YEAR: _____

_____

_____

_____

SEPTEMBER 16

What is your dream car?

YEAR: _____

_____

_____

_____

YEAR: _____

_____

_____

_____

YEAR: _____

_____

_____

_____

SEPTEMBER 17

What is your good-luck charm?

YEAR: _____

_____

_____

_____

YEAR: _____

_____

_____

_____

YEAR: _____

_____

_____

_____

SEPTEMBER 18

What is your biggest fear?

YEAR: _____

_____

_____

_____

YEAR: _____

_____

_____

_____

YEAR: _____

_____

_____

_____

SEPTEMBER 19

What is the bravest thing
you have done?

YEAR: _____

_____

_____

_____

YEAR: _____

_____

_____

_____

YEAR: _____

_____

_____

_____

SEPTEMBER 20

Who hasn't been nice to you lately?

YEAR: _____

_____

_____

_____

YEAR: _____

_____

_____

_____

YEAR: _____

_____

_____

_____

SEPTEMBER 21

What is your nickname?

YEAR: _____

_____

_____

YEAR: _____

_____

_____

_____

YEAR: _____

_____

_____

_____

SEPTEMBER 22

Would you rather take
a bath or a shower?

YEAR: _____

_____

_____

_____

YEAR: _____

_____

_____

_____

YEAR: _____

_____

_____

_____

SEPTEMBER 23

What city is your favorite?

YEAR: _____

_____

_____

_____

YEAR: _____

_____

_____

_____

YEAR: _____

_____

_____

_____

SEPTEMBER 24

How would you describe yourself?

YEAR: _____

_____

_____

_____

YEAR: _____

_____

_____

_____

YEAR: _____

_____

_____

_____

SEPTEMBER 25

If you had a million dollars, what
would you do with it?

YEAR: _____

_____

_____

YEAR: _____

_____

_____

_____

YEAR: _____

_____

_____

_____

SEPTEMBER 26

What did you forget to do today?

YEAR: _____

_____

_____

_____

YEAR: _____

_____

_____

_____

YEAR: _____

_____

_____

_____

SEPTEMBER 27

What do you miss about
last school year?

YEAR: _____

_____

_____

_____

YEAR: _____

_____

_____

_____

YEAR: _____

_____

_____

_____

SEPTEMBER 28

What is your favorite
subject in school?

YEAR: _____

_____

_____

YEAR: _____

_____

_____

_____

YEAR: _____

_____

_____

_____

SEPTEMBER 29

Whom would you hang out with
all day if you could?

YEAR:

YEAR:

YEAR:

SEPTEMBER 30

What is the last thing you ate?

YEAR: _____

_____

_____

_____

YEAR: _____

_____

_____

_____

YEAR: _____

_____

_____

_____

OCTOBER 1

How much money have you saved?

YEAR: _____

YEAR: _____

YEAR: _____

OCTOBER 2

What makes you angry?

YEAR: _____

_____

_____

_____

YEAR: _____

_____

_____

_____

YEAR: _____

_____

_____

OCTOBER 3

What made you smile today?

YEAR: _____

_____

_____

_____

YEAR: _____

_____

_____

_____

YEAR: _____

_____

_____

_____

OCTOBER 4

What toy or stuffed animal have you
kept from when you were younger?

YEAR: _____

YEAR: _____

YEAR: _____

OCTOBER 5

What time do you need to wake
up in the morning?

YEAR:

YEAR:

YEAR:

OCTOBER 6

What do you like to share?

YEAR: _____

_____

_____

_____

YEAR: _____

_____

_____

_____

YEAR: _____

_____

_____

_____

OCTOBER 7

What is the last field
trip you remember?

YEAR:

_____

_____

_____

YEAR:

_____

_____

_____

YEAR:

_____

_____

_____

OCTOBER 8

Is school too easy,
too hard, or just right?

YEAR:

YEAR:

YEAR:

OCTOBER 9

In the fall, I like to

_____.

YEAR: _____

_____

_____

_____

YEAR: _____

_____

_____

_____

YEAR: _____

_____

_____

_____

OCTOBER 10

_____

stresses me out.

YEAR: _____

_____

_____

_____

YEAR: _____

_____

_____

_____

YEAR: _____

_____

_____

_____

OCTOBER 11

Who is your coolest neighbor?

YEAR: _____

_____

_____

_____

YEAR: _____

_____

_____

_____

YEAR: _____

_____

_____

_____

OCTOBER 12

Name something you do really well.

YEAR: _____

_____

_____

_____

YEAR: _____

_____

_____

_____

YEAR: _____

_____

_____

_____

OCTOBER 13

What is your favorite time of day?

YEAR: _____

_____

_____

_____

YEAR: _____

_____

_____

_____

YEAR: _____

_____

_____

_____

OCTOBER 14

I wish I could _____.

YEAR: _____

_____

_____

_____

YEAR: _____

_____

_____

_____

YEAR: _____

_____

_____

_____

OCTOBER 15

What country would
you like to visit?

YEAR: _____

YEAR: _____

YEAR: _____

OCTOBER 16

I am thankful for _____.

YEAR: _____

_____

_____

_____

YEAR: _____

_____

_____

_____

YEAR: _____

_____

_____

_____

OCTOBER 17

What are some of the news
headlines today?

YEAR: _____

YEAR: _____

YEAR: _____

OCTOBER 18

Tomorrow, I will

_____ .

YEAR: _____

_____

_____

_____

YEAR: _____

_____

_____

_____

YEAR: _____

_____

_____

_____

OCTOBER 19

I wish there was a law against

_____.

YEAR: _____

_____

_____

_____

YEAR: _____

_____

_____

_____

YEAR: _____

_____

_____

_____

OCTOBER 20

What do you wish you could tell
your teacher or principal?

YEAR: _____

YEAR: _____

YEAR: _____

OCTOBER 21

What is your favorite snack?

YEAR: _____

_____

_____

_____

YEAR: _____

_____

_____

_____

YEAR: _____

_____

_____

_____

OCTOBER 22

What is your best
memory from last summer?

YEAR: _____

_____

_____

_____

YEAR: _____

_____

_____

_____

YEAR: _____

_____

_____

_____

OCTOBER 23

What is your lucky number?

YEAR: _____

_____

_____

_____

YEAR: _____

_____

_____

_____

YEAR: _____

_____

_____

_____

OCTOBER 24

What is the most annoying thing
that happened today?

YEAR: _____

YEAR: _____

YEAR: _____

OCTOBER 25

What is your favorite song to sing?

YEAR: _____

_____

_____

_____

YEAR: _____

_____

_____

_____

YEAR: _____

_____

_____

_____

OCTOBER 26

Do you want to spend more or
less time with your parents?

YEAR: _____

_____

_____

_____

YEAR: _____

_____

_____

_____

YEAR: _____

_____

_____

_____

OCTOBER 27

What YouTube video
have you watched lately?

YEAR: _____

_____

_____

YEAR: _____

_____

_____

YEAR: _____

_____

_____

OCTOBER 28

What age did you enjoy most, and why?

YEAR: _____

_____

_____

_____

YEAR: _____

_____

_____

_____

YEAR: _____

_____

_____

_____

OCTOBER 29

What is your favorite electronic device?

YEAR: _____

_____

_____

_____

YEAR: _____

_____

_____

_____

YEAR: _____

_____

_____

_____

OCTOBER 30

If you could choose your next family
vacation, where would you go?

YEAR: _____

_____

_____

YEAR: _____

_____

_____

YEAR: _____

_____

_____

OCTOBER 31

What are your Halloween plans?

YEAR: _____

_____

_____

_____

YEAR: _____

_____

_____

_____

YEAR: _____

_____

_____

_____

NOVEMBER 1

If you could have a sleepover
tonight, whom would you invite?

YEAR: _____

_____

_____

_____

YEAR: _____

_____

_____

_____

YEAR: _____

_____

_____

NOVEMBER 2

What is the last photo you took?

YEAR: _____

_____

_____

_____

YEAR: _____

_____

_____

_____

YEAR: _____

_____

_____

_____

NOVEMBER 3

Who is your own
personal superhero?

YEAR: _____

_____

_____

_____

YEAR: _____

_____

_____

_____

YEAR: _____

_____

_____

_____

NOVEMBER 4

Who's the most successful
person you know?

YEAR: _____

_____

_____

_____

YEAR: _____

_____

_____

_____

YEAR: _____

_____

_____

_____

NOVEMBER 5

What has truly surprised you?

YEAR: _____

YEAR: _____

YEAR: _____

NOVEMBER 6

How late do you stay up at night?

YEAR: _____

YEAR: _____

YEAR: _____

NOVEMBER 7

When you are wrong,
what do you do?

YEAR: _____

_____

_____

_____

YEAR: _____

_____

_____

_____

YEAR: _____

_____

_____

_____

NOVEMBER 8

What would be the best job to have?

YEAR: _____

_____

_____

_____

YEAR: _____

_____

_____

_____

YEAR: _____

_____

_____

_____

NOVEMBER 9

What is the coolest
trip you have taken?

YEAR: _____

_____

_____

_____

YEAR: _____

_____

_____

_____

YEAR: _____

_____

_____

_____

NOVEMBER 10

What makes you
work your hardest?

YEAR: _____

_____

_____

_____

YEAR: _____

_____

_____

_____

YEAR: _____

_____

_____

_____

NOVEMBER 11

What is the most hurtful thing
someone has ever said to you?

YEAR: _____

_____

_____

_____

YEAR: _____

_____

_____

_____

YEAR: _____

_____

_____

_____

NOVEMBER 12

Whose advice do you trust?

YEAR: _____

_____

_____

_____

YEAR: _____

_____

_____

_____

YEAR: _____

_____

_____

_____

NOVEMBER 13

What is the last grade you got on a math test?

YEAR: _____

_____

_____

_____

YEAR: _____

_____

_____

_____

YEAR: _____

_____

_____

NOVEMBER 14

What helps you get through a
long school day?

YEAR: _____

_____

_____

_____

YEAR: _____

_____

_____

_____

YEAR: _____

_____

_____

_____

NOVEMBER 15

What makes you feel peaceful?

YEAR: _____

YEAR: _____

YEAR: _____

NOVEMBER 16

What makes you laugh really hard?

YEAR: _____

_____

_____

_____

YEAR: _____

_____

_____

_____

YEAR: _____

_____

_____

_____

NOVEMBER 17

My best friend is the coolest because _____.

YEAR: _____

_____

_____

_____

YEAR: _____

_____

_____

_____

YEAR: _____

_____

_____

_____

NOVEMBER 18

I embarrassed myself
when I _____.

YEAR: _____

_____

_____

_____

YEAR: _____

_____

_____

_____

YEAR: _____

_____

_____

_____

NOVEMBER 19

What instrument would
you like to learn to play?

YEAR: _____

YEAR: _____

YEAR: _____

NOVEMBER 20

How do you help others?

YEAR: _____

YEAR: _____

YEAR: _____

NOVEMBER 21

What did you daydream
about today?

YEAR: _____

_____

_____

_____

YEAR: _____

_____

_____

_____

YEAR: _____

_____

_____

_____

NOVEMBER 22

How important is it to you to
have good grades?

YEAR: _____

_____

_____

YEAR: _____

_____

_____

YEAR: _____

_____

_____

NOVEMBER 23

Life is _____ .

YEAR: _____

_____

_____

_____

YEAR: _____

_____

_____

_____

YEAR: _____

_____

_____

_____

NOVEMBER 24

Which friend invites
you over the most?

YEAR: _____

YEAR: _____

YEAR: _____

NOVEMBER 25

If you could play a joke on anyone
today, whom would you play it on?

YEAR: _____

YEAR: _____

YEAR: _____

NOVEMBER 26

Write a silly poem about your day.

YEAR: _____

_____

_____

_____

YEAR: _____

_____

_____

_____

YEAR: _____

_____

_____

_____

NOVEMBER 27

What are you most excited about this week?

YEAR: _____

_____

_____

_____

YEAR: _____

_____

_____

_____

YEAR: _____

_____

_____

_____

NOVEMBER 28

If you could set a world record,
what would it be?

YEAR: _____

YEAR: _____

YEAR: _____

NOVEMBER 29

What's your favorite way to relax?

YEAR: _____

_____

_____

_____

YEAR: _____

_____

_____

_____

YEAR: _____

_____

_____

_____

NOVEMBER 30

Which is the scariest animal: a
shark, a snake, or a spider?

YEAR: _____

_____

_____

YEAR: _____

_____

_____

_____

YEAR: _____

_____

_____

_____

DECEMBER 1

Who is the bravest
person you know?

YEAR: _____

_____

_____

_____

YEAR: _____

_____

_____

_____

YEAR: _____

_____

_____

_____

DECEMBER 2

My favorite after-school activity

is _____.

YEAR: _____

_____

_____

_____

YEAR: _____

_____

_____

_____

YEAR: _____

_____

_____

_____

DECEMBER 3

The most important thing I have learned
this year is _____.

YEAR: _____

_____

_____

_____

YEAR: _____

_____

_____

_____

YEAR: _____

_____

_____

_____

DECEMBER 4

Today, my mood was

_____ .

YEAR: _____

YEAR: _____

YEAR: _____

DECEMBER 5

If I was president, I would

_____.

YEAR: _____

_____

_____

_____

YEAR: _____

_____

_____

_____

YEAR: _____

_____

_____

_____

DECEMBER 6

If I was invisible, I would

_____.

YEAR: _____

YEAR: _____

YEAR: _____

DECEMBER 7

My favorite website is

_____ .

YEAR: _____

_____

_____

_____

YEAR: _____

_____

_____

_____

YEAR: _____

_____

_____

_____

DECEMBER 8

The easiest subject in school is

_____.

YEAR: _____

_____

_____

_____

YEAR: _____

_____

_____

_____

YEAR: _____

_____

_____

_____

DECEMBER 9

Whom do you get along with
really well in your family?

YEAR: _____

_____

_____

_____

YEAR: _____

_____

_____

_____

YEAR: _____

_____

_____

_____

DECEMBER 10

My happy place is

_____.

YEAR: _____

_____

_____

_____

YEAR: _____

_____

_____

_____

YEAR: _____

_____

_____

_____

DECEMBER 11

What is your favorite hobby?

YEAR: _____

_____

_____

YEAR: _____

_____

_____

YEAR: _____

_____

_____

DECEMBER 12

What drives you crazy?

YEAR:

YEAR:

YEAR:

DECEMBER 13

What do you wish your teacher
would do more often?

YEAR: _____

_____

_____

_____

YEAR: _____

_____

_____

_____

YEAR: _____

_____

_____

_____

DECEMBER 14

What is happening in
your home right now?

YEAR: _____

YEAR: _____

YEAR: _____

DECEMBER 15

Who is your favorite musician?

YEAR: _____

_____

_____

_____

YEAR: _____

_____

_____

_____

YEAR: _____

_____

_____

_____

DECEMBER 16

What are you hoping to avoid today?

YEAR: _____

_____

_____

_____

YEAR: _____

_____

_____

_____

YEAR: _____

_____

_____

_____

DECEMBER 17

When I grow up, I want to be

_____ .

YEAR: _____

_____

_____

_____

YEAR: _____

_____

_____

_____

YEAR: _____

_____

_____

_____

DECEMBER 18

What is your favorite
winter activity?

YEAR: _____

_____

_____

_____

YEAR: _____

_____

_____

_____

YEAR: _____

_____

_____

_____

DECEMBER 19

What is one thing you keep hidden?

YEAR: _____

_____

_____

_____

YEAR: _____

_____

_____

_____

YEAR: _____

_____

_____

_____

DECEMBER 20

What is the best way
to start the day?

YEAR: _____

_____

_____

YEAR: _____

_____

_____

YEAR: _____

_____

_____

DECEMBER 21

Three things I am good at are

_____.

_____

_____

_____

_____

_____

_____

_____

_____

_____

DECEMBER 22

If you could only eat one food for the
rest of your life, what would it be?

YEAR: _____

YEAR: _____

YEAR: _____

DECEMBER 23

Who is the smartest
person you know?

YEAR: _____

_____

_____

_____

YEAR: _____

_____

_____

_____

YEAR: _____

_____

_____

_____

DECEMBER 24

Someone I miss hanging out
with is _____.

YEAR: _____

_____

_____

_____

YEAR: _____

_____

_____

_____

YEAR: _____

_____

_____

_____

DECEMBER 25

What is the secret to a good life?

YEAR: _____

YEAR: _____

YEAR: _____

DECEMBER 26

What is something you know
for sure about yourself?

YEAR: _____

_____

_____

YEAR: _____

_____

_____

_____

YEAR: _____

_____

_____

_____

DECEMBER 27

The last time I had a great idea
was when I _____.

YEAR: _____

_____

_____

_____

YEAR: _____

_____

_____

_____

YEAR: _____

_____

_____

_____

DECEMBER 28

Look under your bed and
describe what you see.

YEAR:

YEAR:

YEAR:

DECEMBER 29

What helps you get
through a tough day?

YEAR: _____

_____

_____

_____

YEAR: _____

_____

_____

_____

YEAR: _____

_____

_____

_____

DECEMBER 30

I deserve an award for

_____.

YEAR: _____

_____

_____

_____

YEAR: _____

_____

_____

_____

YEAR: _____

_____

_____

_____

DECEMBER 31

What is your favorite memory from this past year?

YEAR: _____

_____

_____

_____

YEAR: _____

_____

_____

_____

YEAR: _____

_____

_____

_____